WHITE PETALS FALL UPON ME

White Petals Fall Upon Me

A collection of poems

by

DONNY BARILLA

Adelaide Books
New York / Lisbon
2020

WHITE PETALS FALL UPON ME
A collection of poems
By Donny Barilla

Copyright © by Donny Barilla
Cover design © 2020 Adelaide Books

Published by Adelaide Books, New York / Lisbon
adelaidebooks.org

Editor-in-Chief
Stevan V. Nikolic

All rights reserved. No part of this book may be reproduced in any manner whatsoever without written permission from the author except in the case of brief quotations embodied in critical articles and reviews.

For any information, please address Adelaide Books
at info@adelaidebooks.org
or write to:
Adelaide Books
244 Fifth Ave. Suite D27
New York, NY, 10001

ISBN: 978-1-954351-24-0

Printed in the United States of America

Dedicated to,

Mathew, "Your kindness knows no boundaries

Contents

Mallard and the Instance of Her Touch   *17*

Growth and the Trembling Buds   *18*

Waiting for the Sycamore Tree   *19*

Blue Spruce   *20*

Sauces at the Cabin   *21*

Apples and Pears   *22*

Post   *23*

She Comes to Me in Breads and Seeds   *24*

Leaving the Fields of Wheat   *25*

Birchwood and the Fallen Leaves   *26*

From Forest to Field   *27*

Bread by the Stream   *28*

Donny Barilla

Afternoon *29*

Interruptions *30*

By the Pond *31*

End in the Arms of the Sea *32*

Within the Soils *33*

Rise of the Summer Nymph *34*

Lifting Smoke *35*

Aromas *36*

Meeting an Old Friend on the Mountain Peak *37*

Resting at the Edge of the Woods *38*

I Leave the Mountain Crest *39*

Escaping the Storm *40*

Autumn Rain *41*

After the Pause *42*

Touch of the Fever of Passage at Night *43*

Return from South Mountain *44*

Eastern Flank *45*

Cottons *46*

WHITE PETALS FALL UPON ME

Past the Milkweed **47**

Entering Winter **48**

Wheats and Maize **49**

Winter Fog **50**

Snow Paved Road **51**

Gown of the Earth **52**

Lantern Fades **53**

April Pearls **54**

Into the Pasture **55**

Flesh in the Woods **56**

First Moment of Spring **57**

Sacred Winter **58**

Wading in the Grass **59**

Black of Her Hair **60**

Naked Hickory **61**

Into Nightfall with the Red Tailed Hawk **62**

Winter's Fracture **63**

Wading Thigh Deep **64**

Donny Barilla

Black of Night *65*

Dust in the Moment Before Morning *66*

Second Into Autumn *67*

Weeping Cherry Blossom *68*

Spices and Fragrances *69*

Walking in Pastures *70*

Autumn Search *71*

By the Creek I Hear the Blackbird *72*

Wildhoney *73*

From the Dwelling *74*

Search for Rain *75*

Fading Oak Trees *76*

By the Windowpane *77*

Bread Which Fills the Shadow of the Earth *78*

End *79*

Rise of the Blood *80*

Parting at the Pine Tree *81*

Frozen Fleece *82*

WHITE PETALS FALL UPON ME

Emeralds Speak from the Sky **83**

Alchemy **84**

Through Fields of Wheat **85**

Reach of the Apple Grove **86**

Smash of the Rain **87**

King of the Mustard Seed **88**

Cove **89**

In From the Falling Rain **90**

White Petal **91**

Receding to the Soils of Night **92**

Migration **93**

Goblets and Creek **94**

Days in the Park **95**

Dash of the Gazelles **96**

Into the Bog **97**

Charms and Flocks **98**

By the Lake **99**

Apple Grove **100**

Donny Barilla

In the Chyme of Midnight *101*

Cobalts in the Forest *102*

Vapors along the Velvet Carpet *103*

Hickory Tree *104*

Crown *105*

Warmth *106*

Lilacs *107*

Eulogy *108*

Fields in the Frost of Morning Dampness *109*

Quiver of Night *110*

Past the Hickory Tree *111*

Branch and Twig *112*

Looking upon You *113*

Gazelle *114*

Rain Storm *115*

Molecules *116*

Rib *117*

Lost *118*

WHITE PETALS FALL UPON ME

Falling Petals   ***119***

Wedding Day   ***120***

Fall of the Quilt   ***121***

Autumn Vapors   ***122***

In a Moment   ***123***

Opening Skirt upon the Wild Wind   ***124***

Fertility of the Autumn Woods   ***125***

By the Cabin   ***126***

About the Author   ***127***

Resting beneath the white cherry blossoms,
I gather the petals and place them in suited pouches,
By morning, I glisten the shade of ivory.

Mallard and the Instance of Her Touch

The mallard sliced across the bend of the lake;
youth trimmed the flat gray stones and ran ripples from edge to edge
where the fountain held deep in the center, laughing water.

Where the sand and pebbles stroked the
circumference of the shaking deep
of the water, brisk and blue hues,
I rested upon the poise park bench and
slung my thoughts to the shaded
colors upon the shake of the waters caress and touch.

As I paused in the hour of midday, I shook to
the shears of midnight's trembling gush.
This Summer night groomed warmth upon
the shelter of rain which flushed
deely from the black and lavender cloak of the sky.

We met at the precise moment when we always meet.
The tremors of her cool hands fell brisk upon the paleness of my neck.

In the distance, I heard the stones as they
slapped the trembling, snapping water.

Growth and the Trembling Buds

Angled to the sun, the red maple reached the
width of each surrounding maple
and shone, exposed the medium green buds
which responded to the breeze
and wallowed among the freshest winds
which shook the trembling leaves
across the showered earth which caressed
each leaf across the reach of the
moaning scratch, from bed to blanketed twist of the forest.

I approached the mound of the reds and deepest
purples, sunk beneath the fade of the heavy buds
which sauntered and snapped through the hurry of the winds.

Waist deep in the fluttering spread where the red
parchment scratched each parchment,
I felt the moan of the sky which sizzled my
flesh upon the coolest Autumn air
and fibers of the leaves snipped upon my flesh
as the sun swept behind the clouds.

By the deep fracture of night, I arrived at the
cottage, she hung the cloth and clothing upon
the spread of the line.

She swelled in the canals of her belly as I reached
to her and felt the budding sweet growth
which deepened upon the case and caverns of fruition.

Waiting for the Sycamore Tree

I reach my back, neck against the chapel wall and wash my face
with the dust of the burrowing earth, slung
into the place of restful decline.

Weeping upon me, I feel the winds of the arid fields fumble their way
as the sweetest desert rose tosses each petal upon me.

With a lucent hazel underlying sky, I moan
upon the most clever sweet variation
of fragrances which tumble across the meadow
and draft into my glazes and sweat.

I look upon the narrow stretch of the field and
watch the sinews of her legs and waist
tread and strut to the edges of my flesh, tenderly alive.

We walked to the stretch of the sulking
sycamore and revealed ourselves
upon the empty clothes and gathering leaves.

Blue Spruce

Her thin, threaded voice dashed through the
endless living trees, ferns and soft mosses
as I felt the echo of my bones quiver to
the arrangement of her touch.

With sweet laughter, my spine jumped to a sudden
chill and quickly I sulked upon the root
and the wildflower.

We shared the rib of the earth as the sun sliced
down upon the thinnest of horizons.

I spoke to the pink which pooled upon the gray
slim clouds, I lusted after the thick burgundy
stretch and smiled upon the amber roses
which loomed in precedence.

I reached the stretching row of the blue spruce as
sweetly I found her alive in all her nakedness
and tenderly the fullness of her breasts crowded me in silence.

As we left at the hour of midnight, the needles
spread and depressed upon the ground.

Together in the softness of the earth, I suckled upon
the rain as the heat of Summer softened to a blaze.

Sauces at the Cabin

The cabin held the support of the overstretched eaves
which tossed the swift rain and brought mud to the
hard cake of the earth, readied in the forest.

With my outstretched hand, I felt the
trickle of the snapping rain as it
trickled through finger and promise of the thumb.

With freshness, I tasted the polish of the fumbling
sliver in the gray suckling clouds.

As the crisp sting of the rain ceased, I made
way through the hardest of wood
and sweetly witnessed her in slumber, resting nude upon the bed.

I breathed the wheat of the meadow as I
coddled and swabbed upon her;
tender hours of the chapel, I moved myself
upon the curve of the bending
blouse which held the pouches, nurturing breasts.

Into the fade of midday, I smelled the distant
pat and lusts of the dripping sauce
as I turned to her and flooded upon her.

Apples and Pears

Among the assembly of the oak trees
which stretch and open each bud
in the tremble of the dancing sunlight, I
wash my hands upon the water
so near the flickering creek, I knelt and drank in the blossom of the
awaiting reception where you touch the perfection of my flesh,
moving as a swift pulse of the Spring flavors, apples and pears.

I stood by the moan of the trickling stream with moment past,
I felt the washing breath of the forest chant.

In a quivering second, dashed, I watched
as she waded across the creek,
sat down and soothed my aching legs with the chill of her hand.

We lay upon the flex of ourselves and
spoke upon the thrashing wind.

Post

So angled and far into the depth of the pasture
and the pebbled trim of the country road,
walking the edge of the scarred picket fence, I breathed the winds
of the heavy swab where the gray and charcoal
sky became sliced by the sun
and a sliver and tapping moisture bloomed as a
haze across the surroundings of my full body.

As the moisture ceased,
lost, thirsty and barron, empty, I fell to the
dust which fumbled and coated me
as the sweet mint thrashed across me and
I turned to the fence post and
curled upon the greatness of the arid swift dirt.

I heard the echo of my voice as the resonance
slapped the occasional tree
and tenderly, I faded to the gift of the fellows of the deceased.

She Comes to Me in Breads and Seeds

The sky roamed as crunched scarlett and faded west to a pale pink;
from the north the skies swept in fury as gray and heavy charcoals.

Into the wrestling branches of this Autumn evening, I
lulled into a swerving daydream, leaves collected and soaked
across the body and bust of me.

Into the early hours of night, I stood and recalled the pale breasts she
held upon me as the cream of the wealth of maternity.

You stepped among me as the breads and
seeds of the soaking dampness
of the earth and sweetly trembled the fluids from each nipple and sweat
of your forehead which stung the glazes on the eyes and bodies where
your fullness stripped upon the wedge of
me and my burning slumber
fell in shards,
I trembled to the silk touch of these crimping Autumn quilt
which roamed these quiet leaves.

Leaving the Fields of Wheat

Through the fluid waver, beneath the sauntering wind, I listened
to the wheat as each thread and seed gathered
upon the palm of my hand,
tenderly I thought of her and all swelling rise of the fireplace
which cascaded an auburn hue upon the brim of her flesh.

After I breached the threshold of the cabin which rested in the arms
of oak, I approached the flickering flames and softened upon the
deep slouch of the eager leather chair.

She soothed beside me as I rested my head upon the fullness
of her breasts and slid my fingers across the warmth of her flower,
the covet of the most thoughtful strain of life.

Upon me she sat and we trembled into the
first motion of floods and pastures.

Birchwood and the Fallen Leaves

I slid beneath the shade and loosened to the tossing shadows
of the birchwood which tossed eager scents
and threw them upon me.

The leaves fell upon me and shrouded me
as a blanket threading beneath
the late Autumn hush, scampering through the fading rays of the sun.

I stood and raped the black arms of nightfall which fell; the cool
starving grip of tender and beautiful moonlit
leaves shuddered and gathered
on the ground.

Wearing the sleeves of tapering carpet of the
spread of the regal charm of dinner
and all it's delicacies, I absorbed the entirety
of the forest scent, fragrance.

She slithered across the woods and curled upon my lap
where the gush of the salve united us.

I opened the passage to infancy and washed
every inch of the near creek
which held my feet as the soot trembled and I readied to the kelp
and nectar of the premonition of life.

From Forest to Field

Into the depths of the rich and delicate, blooming forest,
I carve my feet into the laziest of flickering leaves.

Between the heat of my flesh and the press of the flannel
shirt I adorn, the swing of the patterns of the sky emptied
fresh gallons of air upon every patch of
the softest reach of my body.

By the soothing clovers of the dance of the morning draft and all
it's tender floods,

I speak to the living and suckle the breath of the dead
as the fields draw sap upon the marble stone.

I swim through the mineral rich soil as the voice of the dead coiled
around me and welcomed me from the
dark eye of the trembling forest.

Bread by the Stream

Against the pale, fragrant flesh of her, I walked to meet
the fullness of her as the sap of her tender pores swam across me.

I felt the cavern of her stream, river and cove which bent
in the moisture of the living sundance.

Sweet valley's rose as the breath beneath her
breasts and a sauntering fragment
of the milks fed the dampness of the slithering creek.

With the sting of my eyes, I witnessed her
walking to the edge of the brook;
we relished in our nudity as the fullest of
flavors suspended us in touch.

I carved my way upon the sweet moisture
of the heavy press of the meadow.

As night depressed into the giant welt of the swooning passages,
I carved into the spirit of the laughter of
the taste of the bread of her.

Afternoon

I held her hand as a delicacy, sweet aromas,
roses and lilacs dance from her neck,
I press my lips upon her and swoon with the tumbling wind.

I felt the warmth of her seasoned blood which
flushed to the depth of my groin and all
it's arousal.

As we lay upon the tender grip of the darkest green mosses,
I place my hand upon the full pouch and the
smooth breads which pause upon my lips.

She slept along the torso of my body and the rains screamed and slid
along the mud of the forest floor; I spoke
of the living and wept for the dead
as the sky proclaimed innocence. I heard
the bones, so deep in the earth,
choke upon the marrow of each bone.

By afternoon, the pounding slash of the press of
the sky relished upon the carved brittle trees
and the saunter of the returning heat.

I look upon you in all your fullness and nakedness.

Interruptions

As I walk through the red maples, I smile
upon the scarlet crunch of the eager
scattered press of the most collected leaves.

Moisture of the floods which swept and hurried across
the fullness of the pounding and slapping stream,
opened the madness of the trembling winds.

I listened to the moaning charisma of the
vowels and verbs as they tossed
droplets of pearls into the reach of this slant
and looseness where the driftwood
sliced and filled with rapids and foams.

Reaching into the canopy of the crowded treetops,
I huddled beneath the trees and leaned upon the
trunk as the honey and patches of mint
swam to the bridge of my nose and filled me with life.

I waited for the next dance of the sunrise which
shook every hue; sweet pastures led me to her,
alive among the barns and slant of the fields of
wheat, we rest and coddle with each
scream of every genitals.

By the Pond

She slipped through the film of the curve of the pond;
Her hair motioned forth as a sheet of silk
slouched and slithered across her shoulders and
reached down the paleness of her back.

She rose from the slender pouch where kelp and soot traced across
The velvets of her sweet tender breasts.

Every satin sheet of the haunch and dip caressed her in fabrics, cool
Slippery wind tangled upon her as the
summit of her breast spoke to me
The depths of Autumn.

I stand so near, the oak leaf slipped through the pollens
Which dripped along every quiver of bead and rippling crush.

I took her into the softness of my hands and
sauntered along with the crushed velvets
Which sweetened in glazes of her foamed cove.

End in the Arms of the Sea

I gently spoke of the foamed waves which sang to you and crashed
with weeping verbs along the towering cliffs as the prism of the sun
wept in showers across the edge of the sea,
trellising hues of endless colors,
I felt you upon the fullness of my pale skin.

You spoke of dampness which swelled
across the fluids of the flickering
eddies and the burn where the touch of you stung to the chill
of my pounding veins.

Upon the ending waves of the quivering
passages of the sweet taste of the ocean,
I dove, fell as a vapor and trembled beneath the dancing light.

I return to the pebbles of the kelp which chant each slithering descent,
softly I carve upon the bedding of the floor of the sea
which quivers the motions of my flesh and I coarse my passage upon
the shrouding black arms of the deep.

Within the Soils

Upon the most slender path to the most emerald meadow,
I walk to the triumph of the oak tree which
shadows the limbs with blackbirds.

Upon hearing the branches crackle with the passages of wind,
I speak to the press of the acorn and hear the dancing sun.

Six months ago at this moment, I curved and
engulfed the shout of the spirited
thunder which tangled with the crimson sky;
I touch the falling leaf and covet the softest
press of eager, spreading grass.

I lay upon the base of the trunk where the roots deepen.
the sweet flavors of your perfumed neck rise with the taping rain.

I hear you quiver with the polished glaze of the suckling soil
and minerals of the suckling soil.

Rise of the Summer Nymph

I lean upon the rising blend of Summer grass,
stroked to the top of the summit.
Jades, emeralds, soft hues of the weed and glint of the clover leaf,
I gather every tender scent as the smoke
rose to the lowering mist and fog.

I look into the deep chasms of the sulking
valley which grazes every tamp
of each foot which suckles moisture upon the
heavy threads where the strong women
wade deeply upon the quivering chill of the river, pond and lake.

I speak in softness as the shivering nymph
held the slithering streaming water
tenderly upon the breasts which motioned and purred.

I return to the deep of the grass and in the swift seconds of madness
I carve my way upon the bloom of the sweet
trembling breeze, fondling upon the
growth of the sauntering blades.

Lifting Smoke

I watch the smoke lift from the rock and shoulders, rise from the peak
of South Mountain as the voices of the
majestic winds scream of triumph and
treasures which follow the rain.

The earth slouched alive in the dampness of the
threads of the Summer posture and grip.

As I stand alone in this trembling wind,
I feel her breath soothe and coddle me as vapors of the scattered trees
holding the suspension of the sweet rising prism.

Aromas

Stopping by the curl of the tender green pond,
the sweetest fragrance of the peach rose filled
my lungs with the most aromatic
tug and fervent slant.

At the moment, two years past,
I left her here and heard her sob as the
grass snapped beneath my feet.

As I walked swift and bold,
I became eager upon the patch of the mint
and the falling bark of the birchwood.

Here in the gush of the kelp and the slithering green film,
the ripples of the pond water spoke of her
nakedness and trembling sorrow.

Meeting an Old Friend on the Mountain Peak

Beyond the ivory clouds, the canvas of early day
swelled as the deep purples of a plum
and blended and wrangled with every shade of pink.

The tans and browns, this dusting of dirt and clay
earth rose to the moans of my weakening
feet as I fell upon the roadside and soothed my
eyes with the spread of the tender skyline.

Swiftly, I found the steep crawl of the mountain pass and stepped
deeply upon the rise and cliffs far to the north.

His thatched roof hut spoke with the swarming wind
as the grass blades speared along each inch of the flesh
where he sat, alive in the thinning air of Autumn.

Resting at the Edge of the Woods

With the spoken words of the fall of the heaviest of the oak branch,
I snapped to the grip of the moaning earth and stood for a brief
moment, then swept to the creek where the
fallen wood settled and moistened.

Far into the cascade of the sweet fragrances of the meadow,
I lay upon the mesh of grass, clover and mint.

She lay, rested upon the velvets of the roaming leaves which spread
from the nearby woods.

I soothed and suckled the dampness of her perspiring neck as the ices
of her fingers called upon the fastening
moans which coil through the wind.

I Leave the Mountain Crest

The swift gushing warmth of the dense moaning
forest which stretched and patterned
across the damp breath of the earth, trembled
pearls of sweat as a cotton shirt
depleted and suckled as paste upon the heat of my flesh.
I angled for the top and peak of the iced mountain crest.

Seized upon the frozen tread where the soils, your gift to
the striking winds which passed and threaded beneath the
ice cakes which reach the highest summit and groove of the
apex where you lay, I rest and breath your fragrances which
gust across the depth of the mountains slouching cliffs.

Looking to the white glaze of the sky, I hear the scream of the hawk
which relishes upon the prison of the flesh and all solid defeat.

I turn and search for the blaze of the Summer sun.

Escaping the Storm

I spoke to the rising temper of the wind which
swept and cloaked and coddled across me.

I felt the establishment of the warm blood
which throttled through my veins
as the tender consonants and vowels gathered their perfect speech;
with each heavy taste of the dancing grass which
taunted the soil upon the thickness
of the meadow, I rose above the rising
hill which soothed upon the depths of the edge of the woods
and carved a single path, riddled in acorns and pinecones.

Now, softly placing my feet upon the softest stretch of the earth,
alive in these fragrant soils and minerals, I heard the snapping
and cracking of the wood, high upon the wild treetops.

Now evening, the wine colored sky emptied itself upon
the horizon where the forest crumbled with age.

Autumn Rain

I shook into the presentation of the Autumn rain.
The sapling trembled with fear as the soft, lime colored buds flickered
swiftly into the gush of the seething wind.

Across the canvas of the deeply gray sky,
I could hear the endless choir of the madness
where treasures and charms
cast their shadow of pearl beads for rain.

I gather the aroma of the dying trees, hickory and elm.
with twists of soil and fallen limbs, the earth
danced in preludes and fugues,'

Gently, this course altered and led me to the deeper cry of the earth,
sweetly spoken pastures filled with the sweetest bloods from the depth
of the cracked bones beneath the land upon which I stand.

After the Pause

Upon the burn of the boulders and jagged rocks, I softened myself
into the pause, then rising wind which absorbed
the tamp of the slithering heat
which threaded through each black strand
of hair and every tension of muscles
depleted with the fading journey, I fell upon the
sands of the stretching field of rocks.

Well shaken and quivering upon this summit and mountain peak,
I watched the glazes of orange and the
sweat of the tangerine which
deepened and sank to the writing purple
plums, loosened through the depth
where the cloak of the last fade of day wrapped across me in rhythms.

By the shower of the midday sun,
I fade in dust and soak upon the sweetest marrow of every bone
as the motions of the fallen leaf trembles upon the curve of my ribs.

As I roam with the course of the wrapping wind,
I speak of the continuity of the slicing blades of age as a gentle cool
gush slips through me as sweet verbs answer my call.

Touch of the Fever of Passage at Night

She spread with a flicker of the Autumn
leaves and came to me as the dance
of the waltzing light of the warm, yet distant sun.

Endless needles of the pine tree slouched upon
the rigid earth as I soothed and sulked
with the cherry tree and all white blossoms
which gently took to the sky
as the host, the thickets and green pastures,
spoke of the meadow and dying wheat.

Standing from the trunk of the pine, I breathed
inward and walked perfectly to the moans and
cries of the meadow as I faded with the groom of every seed.

By nightfall and it's velvet cloak, I held the
gusts of the chill of the October night.

As night grew into the depth of the spears of tall blades of grass,
I slowly enter the fevers of this wild touch.

Return from South Mountain

The smoke rose from the tip of the climb of South Mountain
as I gathered the fog which flickered gently across my feet and legs.

The moss spread with peppered moisture as the
sweet color of the midsummer grass
tangled in the hues of emerald and boasted
of the sweat which lurked upon
the highest reach of boulders and rocks.

The air thinned with the writhe of a
serpentine which slipped and curved
deeply into the pouches of my lungs.

With the feel off my trembling feet as I wound
down the path, leading to the soft gestures of the
meadow, I watched as the crows slanted across the
mountain and swarmed in flecks of fading black.

I stood still and spoke to the approach of the
warm gales which flooded each of the grass
blades as the meadow hushed; upon reaching the meadow
I bathed in the fragrance and aromas of the patterns
of each thicket and bush unraveled before me.

Eastern Flank

Upon the patio, fading and chipped paint
the color of pale white, I stood
with the steaming bristling coffee black and watched the rose
colored slip of the soothing blend of the skyline.

I shed my reason with the distant long shadows from the sun;
turning into the crisp chill of the western flank,
I watched the ivory blankets flood each curve and whisper.

I left the cabin with the aching spread of trimmed, spikes of ice.

With great speed, I chased the eastern blood of the skyline.

Cottons

Threads of the willow tree wrapped and coddled
beneath the bashful and cool Autumn sun
which tangled and spoke a humble light upon me.

As the coiling branches tapped and purred upon
the weeping pink hues of my tender flesh,
I softened to the cottons which relish the
joust of the sweeping breath.

The probing gush of the near creek softly
begged for the edges of my feet
as the trembling caress of the rippling eddies pooled across me.

I turned to the fracture of the sky and hosted
a chilled broth upon me as the brook
wavered to the flickering dance of the most remote sunshine.

Past the Milkweed

Stepping aside of the milkweed, this thick stalk tugs upon the sweet
flavors of the suckling scents of touch and procreation.

As your cream colored legs wade through the tender speech
of the rattling winds and the deep of the lime colored meadow.

Walking, I can feel the fullness of your powdered breasts
which resorts to the milk which trembles and trickles,
born of the bread which tangles upon you.

Now evening, the sky lit like a fire, bleeding
reds, oranges and the pale peach;
I look upon the burgundy of her fleshy full skin.

Into the darkness of the sweet green woodlands,
we fade upon the scent of pine trees and the touch of each tender sap.

Entering Winter

Beneath the warmth of her pale, well postured
body, within the bloods off her
trembling veins and tissues which heave in
perfect fassions, I can witness the melt
of the snowflakes as we steep through the
tangle of the frost of the woods,
I place my warm palm upon the snow of her full, black hair.

The pond held rhythms of sweet flavors and
rippling circles as the powdered
snows tap upon the surface and freezing kelp.

With wind gushing in a full breath,
I watch the smoke rise upon the iced, rocky
summit of the nearest mountain peak.

Leaving the thick of the woods,
I entered the pasture and the tallest grass
which led way to the mountain trail;
sweetly, I stamp my feet upon the first dredge of snow as the
green blossomed to a Winter yellow and crust of the dirt.

Wheats and Maize

Watching the full, long gentle hair whipping
through the snapping gusts of wind,
each reaching branch crackled in heavy, gnashing limbs.

She stepped upon the moss and dark green ferns which softened
the walking and tender motion of her fluid edge.

I breathed the scent of her loosening blouse as
the sweet milk filled silence of her breasts
wave as the threaded leaves which gather around her.

With sweats of her abdomen and the tense flicker of her inner thighs,
I covet these sweetened slopes of flesh and the
distant wave of wheat and fields of maize.

Winter Fog

I slept upon the breast and shoulder of her as the moonlit
flicker of the Autumn deepening fall of
leaves guided her hands upon me.

Cool as the trembling ice on the December hollytree,
she swam through the full stretch of my hair as I
eased into her, fullness and gentle fog roamed
along the crossed legs of her
with moisture upon our fleshy full, lips.

I felt the warmth of her breasts as I faded
to the sweet stretch of slumber.
by the red glazes of morning,
I rose to meet her as the fog lifted and she vanished into the depths
of the rising sky.

Snow Paved Road

The soft, slightly frozen puddles, glazed
across the mud, cakes of the earth,
stretched along the slippery road which carved
it's way into the reach of the meadows
and flat whistling winds which spun across the
defeat of each grass blade and spear.

Walking along the frosted, threaded stones which
protrude through the frozen earth and
moans of the soothing search of Spring triumph.

I lift my eyes to the charcoal gray sky and duck beneath the oak tree
which held my stature in the coated gloves
of tender warmth which, pressed
the engulfing snarl of the winds and approach
of the madness in Winter fleece.

By the shadow of the deepest hour of night's darkness, I
surrender to the realm of tender glazes and sweet frosts.

Gown of the Earth

She parted her mouth and I
spoke of the Spring, lush green grasses, which flooded me in the rise
of my warming blood which entered the thrash of my heart
and suckled upon the velvets of the dark night's glaze.

I ran the coarseness of my thumb, finger and palm
with a slow swipe across the fleece of her sweet tender back.

As the gentle fragrance of the floods of Spring rain fell and danced
with a lusty tap of the bead and sweet lights
which flickered into the dressing
gown of the groaning earth, I touched fondly upon you.

Lantern Fades

I sat in the dark wood covered room, as I
watched the candles and lanterns fade;
each smack of each trembling window, resounded across the cottage.
room and glazes in empty light
I heard the flickering, pounding raindrops, slithering
across the window and wooden pane.

Gently, I speak to the quivering of my lips as the shadow
shrouds the room and glazes in empty light.

Into the sudden path of the heaviest of winds,
I walk into the black cloak of the trembling forest,
filled with puddles and pouches of rain.

By morning, I walked in a sudden grip of
ivory skies and reds and rose hues
which soak in moisture and the prism in the water bead.

April Pearls

Into the bloom of pollen and seeds, lofting across the fields of April
and the dancing petals wavering from each cherry blossom;
I stood in silence and spoke to the eager motions of the moist earth.

I spoke with the approaching meadow and
stones as they gathered in the pasture
which stand as a madness between earth and the sweeping sky.

I turned and walked through the flavors of the trees and bushes.
opening my lungs, the bath of the fragrant
dew beads upon each lance of grass and tender weed, I sweetly kissed
the posture of the newest naked pearl, trickling across the quiet meadow
and suckling root of every wildflower.

Into the Pasture

I shook with the quiet winds of this Autumn hush
as the full, gathering of the red maple held a weakening posture
to the bend of the branch and a sweet flavor of the defeated wood
and a cry of the wildflower which trembles in scattering leaves.

The sky became damp as did the floor of the moaning woodlands.

I approached her on the southern bend where the wilting woods
open in a press of the spreading field which dressed itself in seeds
and the gathering of pollen.

I pressed my hands across the inches she opened before me
as I dampened into the warmth of her moisture
and the glaze of her thighs.

Now Winter, I turned and looked to the emptiness of the hollow
of the wild snow patted woods. Gently, I heard her moan.

Flesh in the Woods

I shared breath and spoke to you of the
youth of the early apple and the red,
burgundy cloak of the sky.

I tenderly walk upon the aged relishing
mulch and the carve of every root.

I stood in the splinters of the woods which
held the wild, smacking branches
which shed every portion of the maple and
the towering reach of the hickory tree.

I snapped the flesh of her upon the skin
of the fruit, soft upon the pine
needled spread on the earth covered woodland floor.

I spoke again to the deep shout of the dark threads
of the shadows of the crunching moonlight.

First Moment of Spring

The sky opened in ribbons of yellow and the heaviest of golds;
I walk across this stretch of woods as the softest green felt of the earth
Swept softly beneath my feet.

Passing a stretch of pines which reached across me in sap and draped
Across me in edges of the falling needles, the loosening of the cone,

Fog fell upon the peak and spread of the roaming trees.

After loosening my vest, I stepped upon the fields, meadows and tender
Gush of the jade spread of the pasture, I walk into the endless mist
As the smoke of the soil and grass fell upon the haze of the hills,
Softening in the rise of the sun.

Sacred Winter

Into the depths of this sacred Winter, I gather every aroma and spice
which blends across the frozen dirt and halts the quivering dust.

With silence and patience, the nimble spread of the frost climbs
the gnarled bark of the reaching branches,
crackling upon the December breath.

I reach the hollow of the woods as the moss flakes in heaviness
of the falling groom and bride which fills with fog and takes flight
upon the sweetness of each berry of the
holly bush, snipped by the robins
whom leave the burrowing haunch and sculpt
the path in the softest gestures.

By nightfall, the early spread quivers and
floods the quivering crimson haze.
softened, the dashing snow roams upon each trig and quivering ferns.

Wading in the Grass

Snap of the silent bud wrestles upon the
trembling stretch of the breeze
which echoes across the open plains, a soft mumbling
to the dusty quivering tree branches and
shelter among the tall, edged grasses.

Into the dormancy of the mud, chalk and cake of the earth,
I wade through the steep rise of the bamboo shoots and waver
of the thickness of the onion root which caresses with a heavy scent.

Looking to the rise of the earth and the rise of the distant hills
which tremble their emerald green flourishing hues as a dampness
upon the blade and patch.

Upon the reach and slope of the summit,
I groom my eyes and begin this mesh, moment as the fog and clouds
deepen upon the rising crest.

Most gently, I slant and walk across the
depths of the valley's crooning winds.

Black of Her Hair

Reaching full as the adornment of the
trembling film and kelp of the pond,
I watched in witness, The nakedness of her
and the perfection of her breasts
which slithered beneath the edge of the floods of the water,
I sauntered toward her in restless growth and
tensing slouch of the black pasted hair
which slithered across her back.

Solvently, I thrust and emptied myself into
the distant wheats of the dancing
sun as the pale white thighs trembled upon the groom of my hands.

Wrapping her in the silks which shiver against the afternoon winds,
I can smell the fibers of the leaves which crumble upon the branches
and glaze in dust across the surrounding forest floor.

Naked Hickory

The haze of the flooding wealth of the heaviest grooming sun
flickered and danced upon the fibers of
the field which blended softly
to the roaming looseness of the meadow.

Feeling the tamp of my boots, I sank and waded through the patches
and gestures of the wavering wheat, I reach my stride in miles as the sweet
flavors gripped the senses and tastes as the slithering paints and hues

stripped across the paleness of my approaching nakedness.

I stopped in the handsome shade of the tall,
reaching branches of the hickory tree.
With a common frequency, the scents of the risen joust upon the sky
fell back upon me as the tapping soft rains
nurtured and spoke in perfect silence.

Into Nightfall with the Red Tailed Hawk

Walking the rock strewn and gathering of pebbles on the press
of this aching country road, I witnessed
the rise of the smoky fog which
crept and lounged upon the pine woods upon
the dampness of Blue Mountain;

the red tailed hawk stabs through the mists and glazes of the drifting,
loafing webs which kneels upon the high perch and cleft of the edge.

Following this trembling tamp of my tender feet, I sulk and gasp
upon the rugged trail, slithering to the perfect peak.

Reaching this apex and quiver of the thinning
air, I breath the spreading patches of mint
and rest beneath the blue spruce.

By nightfall, I became clothed in the dance
of the fallen cloak and cloth.

Winter's Fracture

I grazed my hands across the moist, cool spread of clover
with the sweet scent of melting snows of the broken fields
where Winter remains tackled by the warmth of the flood and prune
of the sun grooved upon the earth.

Deep traces of the eager tamp of the slide of the foot, I watched the
tread burrow to the endless glisten of the evergreen woods.

Listening to the song of the blackbird which suspended upon the press
of this wild gasping threads of air, I follow to
the hollow and abundance of the nearby
wildflowers which sulk the center of this wood and praise
as a sweet dancing flock which darts to the treetops and then aims
upon the tender field and meadow.

Into the fracture of the Winter fleece, I
soften and enter a solvent of the Spring
trembling toss of needles and cones.

Wading Thigh Deep

The swift river conquers the flooded fields as the grasses
hold posture to the deepening, billowing
spreads of roots and the spears
of grass which slice the gushing gnash of rain.

I recall her wading thigh deep through the depths of this mad river.

I shook upon the shadows of her breasts
and the wheat trim of her warmth
which softened the chill of her to the
freshness which sliced and fractured
the heavy prism of the river, steep of the sky.

In a slicing river and the madness of the
curve where the edge and bank
roam across the meandering fog with the
swabbing press of the morning mist.

Leaving, I recall the icy touch of her wet fingers which cross through
the sweat and rhythms of the snapping winds of the sky.

Black of Night

I cast my vision leagues deep across the black of the wood
and the smoke covered grays of the sinking sky which flooded upon
this forest so fresh with flavors and scents.

With trembling dampness, the quivering
droplets of pearl colored dew
shook across the slouch of my shoulders.

Walking across the bank of the mud cloaked country road,
I felt the soft breeze soothe the edges
of my face and thrash wildly upon the looseness of my tender hair.

The sky thickened to the shade of a plum
and the spread of the tangerine
threads across the horizon.

By the sweeping black shove of the darkness
of night, I fade among the dusts
which freshen into the sweet of the woods.

Dust in the Moment Before Morning

Soft slumber and I awoke with the tender cloth upon the nakedness
of your most eager twitch and the palest
floods of powder upon your body.

Upon the breads of your pillowed breasts, I fell into you as the sweet
warmth of your flooding thighs began to thrive
along your bushels of trim wheat.

Looking at the defeat of the slump and
drizzled remains of the candles,
I touched you in the shiver of the ending
of the deepest hour of night.

By the slice of morning, I
looked to the dust which hung and glazed slowly
across the tremble of the quiet room.

Second Into Autumn

Standing before the muscle of the oak
and the aroma of the cedar tree,
gently, I recall the fullness and flesh, you sweetly rest
by this gathering of trees, soft among their
tender roots which wrap across
and cultivate you as a meld of the earth.

Into the first moment of the first second of Autumn, I shiver
as this tanned leaf softly falls upon the glazes of the earth.

Weeping Cherry Blossom

I saddled below the weeping cherry blossom,
cool winds stroke and suckle upon my
gentle, loose chestnut brown hair.

I watch the sky sweep in dark grays from the north;
with a long awaited dance of the toss of
leaves and sharp white petals.

As most tender, the soft flower strokes and taps
upon the eager spread of my flesh;
I hear the trickling poise of the most maternal rains

as they soften and feed the crusts of the awaiting earth.

The gripping sky eased as a surmounting
quake upon the sadness of the earth,
tenderly, this sulking open meadow pause with a shout.

Spices and Fragrances

Spices loafe upon the lingering spread of the burlap blanket;
now, the window cracked, I moan upon the
sweet flavors of the melding breeze.

Caramels fill the vacancy of my tender lungs and curl deeply
into the swimming tastes which meander through my spooling mind.

Standing, I place the pants upon me and
deepen into the cove and threads
of my cotton shirt.

Looking back, across my shoulders, I watch her
as she sleeps, slumbers in the pressing
crisp linens caressing and conforming across
her damp, warm body and flesh.

Leaving the white cottage, I deepen and stride upon the fumbling seeds
which dart and dash across the perfect trembling meadow.

Most gentle, I conform to the rise of the
clutching softness of the earth

I relish each fragrance which speaks silent from
the pausing gush of the beginning
speed of tender rain.

I shut my eyes and I absorb her in the shadows of my mind.

Walking in Pastures

Into the steps of the gushing rain, I walk
with the push of my tender feet;
with the backward lean of my swirling
head, I motion with the pressing
glaze of my head, hair so alive in motions
where the touching, loose tremble
of the soft breath of air kneels upon me.

With the crimping touch of her flooded hands,
I dance to the patterns of the pounding
wind searching gently through me.

Softly alive, the suckling groom of the falling leaves,
I spoke to her in patterns of the wilting leaves August past.

Eager, I respond in the thriving whip of the
edged leaves grazing in madness.
quietly, I walk through the softest mud of the softest pasture.

Autumn Search

With the voices of the deep of night, I hear
the threads of the maple dash and tremble upon the hush of the grass.

Tenderly, I walk through the vapors of
the saunter and rise of the cool,
bashful breeze, alive in this pampering loose leaf.

Looking upon the lime colored earth, I softened away to the passages
where the oak spreads in solitude and the quest for Octobers breath.

The gentle slope of the crest and curving
shadow where she slumbers by night,
I speak gracefully upon the sloping paleness of her quivering flesh.

In the moaning grip of her pausung hands,
sweet gusts of flavors soak upon me as the torrent washes among us.

By the Creek I Hear the Blackbird

Evening, the sky stretched alive with fevers
from pink to a fading purple
which sulked across the temoring search of the blanket of black night.

Slow, I walk the edge of the purr of the soaked rocks and kelp
of the dance of the patterns of the creek.

I looked to the sky and spoke of the tremble
of the plush of the sweetest rains;
by the midland crush of the darkest hour, I soak beneath you.

I enter the coo of the morning reach of the blackbird
as the quart glimmers the rising peak of the swarm of the creek.

Wildhoney

With a gentle walk, I pass the webs of this fine mist,
along the soft touch, my skin slithers as the finest silk.

Pearls of swollen dewdrops tap upon the finest
spread of mud and slithering grass.
listening to the chant of every cricket, the choir of the locust,
I swallow the sap and the wildhoney.

Now, well upon the depth of the meadow, I
suckle the breads of this wandering
woman dense through the quivering flower
and widesnip of clover which
tucked and gathered beneath her feet, we
met upon the peak of a rising slope.

I gathered her into the buckle of my thick hands and the dance
of my burrowing lips which open us to the
floods of the darkest gray clouds.

From the Dwelling

From the dwelling, I slouch and hide against
pounding wind which speaks
of tenderness here with the fragrance of every
cedar tree reaching in the dark
of the woodlands.

With travel, I motion and tremble my feet,
quick loosening of these leather boots;
into the fullness of these perfect cedar
woods which a joust to the sky
which spreads heavy as the fall of the smoky
breath in descent of the fumbling clouds.

Speaking to her in the speed and swell of the aromas,
I gently pass my palms along the moisture
puckering along the flat of my knuckles and palms.

As I follow you, I hear the speech and voice
of the earth which fondle me
in the hour of the black shaking the treetops.

Search for Rain

The richness of this kingdom held the wealth
of the sweet maples, red maples.
I spoke to the pines and walked swift upon
their needles, groomed path
as the blitz of the sun warmed me and
splashes burgundies across my face,
my shoulders and the fullness of my torso.

I stopped among the well spread hyacinth and
the soft speech of the darkest fern which
fastens to the wild breach of the pastures burning in the sun.

Having left the quiver and heavy banter of
the trembling madness of the forest,
I crimped the dead moans of defeat of every
blade and stalk of the onion root.

Gently, I placed the cotton and denim across
the shaking crimsons of my skin.
Where in the thick distance of the burning sky,
I walk forever to the shout of the flooded
hills which gather the rains where the clouds
caress both peak and threaded trees.

Fading Oak Trees

Leaving the pond near stretches of the scattering of the oak trees,
alive and tender, the bark whimpers beneath the sweet rain.

Dampness of the quivering green upon the slope of the hills,
motions of the descending marble gray clouds shook heavy winds

across the depths of the valleys and swarming
with the base of the mountain
each which carves the trails to the summit of the mask of night.

Along with the sulking press of fog and trim of passing mist,
the streams flood and thicken with the
edge of mud and eager leaves.

As I look across the crest of my shoulder,
I stand blind to the fade of the oak
trees and fasten the rains upon the tip of my lips and tongue.

By the Windowpane

I tucked in the roots of the finely patterned stalks of wheat,
Cove of my hands shook upon the softest of thighs.

Placing myself upon her lips, ice of her
lips quivered me to the madness
of the down feather pillow, we sank upon
both breasts and the abdomen

which deepens between us and the bed floods in chestnut hair.

By heavy, dark night, we hear the cherry blossom make declarations
with the branches rattling the wood paned window.

I loosen to the quivering gnarled hook of her nakedness
and the fullness of the doughs of her silent flesh covered milks.

Bread Which Fills the Shadow of the Earth

Well stepped across the groove of the
downward slant of the rising hill,
I sweetened my sight and caught a slither
of her as the long stretch of black
trembling shadows, I followed until the shatter of this Summer day.

You fade into the pauses of evening and thick
our way through the tender woods.

With a swift moment before the descension of the pinks and reds
caress the fullness of the earth, I watch
soothingly as the vapors of her

Weakened and sank upon the sulking twist of deep night.

By morning I had lost this journey to the
thinning gasp of carve of the knife
which fills the forested hill with the breads of this
quivering bread, so alive in the warmth
of the sauces of the earth.

End

I reach the cool spread of the slight frost of the moss,
the deep of November floods and scars the chiseled root wedges

softly upon the dredge of the silent fleece of the earth.

Into the passage of the curling warmth of
the sun, feeding the soil and grass
on a sparse occasion, having left the soil which flood,
the genuflect of the sweeping winds carry me with the dust
of the renewal of the earth.

I fasten upon the breasts of the earth which
tremble upon the mountain peaks
and drip into the woods, pampered in evergreens.

Rise of the Blood

I breathe the air from the moisture and fragrance of her gasping lungs;
with posture and grip of the neighboring
window which rattled upon the edges,
I soon flooded the bedroom with chilled breezes,

Longing for the heat of this quivering flesh, I sank upon the sauces
which roam and steep the groom of her soft thighs.

I lean across her and hold likelihood to the
rhythms of the swoon and charm
in which the finches dart upon the tall, heavy
sweep of the darkest of red maples.

I kiss her as the blood rises and floods upon
me in the dance of the trembling sky.

Parting at the Pine Tree

As we lay upon the blanket, riddled in roots where the tender soils
of this fullness where the meadow soothe us and cast shadows

far across the glades, I soften my way to
the coolness of her moisture and
heavy breathe swam in the youth of my warming lips.

She spoke with gestures and postures as the cloth and threads she wore
fell upon the grass of the earth.

Tenderly, I listened to the smashing and crackling branches;
the wind swept through the balding trees as I
moaned for the treasures of her sacred bud.

We walked to the meadows edge and parted with the sweetest smell
of the pine tree which sulked and gathered
cones and needles upon the soft soil.

Frozen Fleece

Standing upon the fields of the ripe gnashing teeth
with stones open to the bite which spread as the jagged comb,
so tenderly alive the thicket and thorns buried
into the soil and crust of the earth.

I surpassed the winds and walked nimble and
slow as the forest swarmed gently
around me.

Leaves gathered as the threads of the spool,
tossing and laying as a fleece
with fine late frost and the tremble of Autumn end.

Bone and marrow of the earth wrapped in
ice and freeze of the chipping layers
of crust, cake and the once softest torte, I
stood and made way for the absence
where the sun pounds upon the drip of the earth.

Emeralds Speak from the Sky

I wander through the cedar wood forest and fill the pouches
of my lungs which absorb fragrances pooling
and spreading through the gentle breeze.

Walking beside the depths of the curl of the sweetest moaning rivets
where the gushing blue waters stroke across the rocks, I listen,

I speak upon the dancing stream of the tunnels of driftwood;
upon drinking the ice chill of the slip of the coasting water,

with full awareness, I step closer to the crawl
of the red skyline which glazes
the meadow with perfect gems, alive in greens and blues in the sweetest

tap upon the host of these emeralds, the spread of carpeted green felts,
I stand to hear the slap of the wind softly speak my name.

Alchemy

Asleep, I hear the shiver of the rib which circled the clay
deepened into the fullness of the earth
and fleshy posture of the earth.

I drink the milk of the sky as sweet breasts polish upon me.
As the sweat of her muscles and tender
motions of her sweet abdomen

and the brisk enhancing alchemy of her wheats and thighs;
I speak to the graves of her empty womb.

Through Fields of Wheat

Softly the glades carried under the pigments
of cherry red and glazed pinks.

Wheats nestled upon my thighs and calves as the breath of this Autumn
sky took my hickory colored hair well into flight.

Upon pressing the motions of my thoughts of her, I became glorified
well into the drip of afternoon.

Next, at the earliest moments of morning,
I suckled upon the nearest creek;
I thought of her as this crisp drink guided
me to the open blouse and thin skirt

Which thickens my groin and pulls me to
the touch of her which swooned
last Summer in the madness of last Summer.

From a distance, the trembling fields of wheat
paused upon the yielding breath of the sky.

I stepped through the grains and wandered my way home.

Reach of the Apple Grove

With the trickling soft rains which flutter
through the moonlit leaves,
I arrange myself and walk clearly to the purr
of the sweet, warm, hot springs.

Nearby, I breath the pollens of the most tender cherrywood;
with a gush of the winds, white blossoms sweep upon the breeze,
the tremble of the passing winds danced upon me.

I walked further and suckled the flesh
of the apple which had fallen
in the shroud of the shadow at evening, the sweet apple grove
pronounced her soft tenderness in the
pastures of the hollow of the wood.

Smash of the Rain

I reach with arms spread and capture the dust of each fallen
branch and the shiver of every leaf.

Rain peppered across the pale, thin exposure of my youthful flesh;
silently, I wander through the mud, filled wash of the meadow.

The rain tamped as a fist from the lowering gray marbled clouds
which sweeten and suckle the buds and pods of Spring.

With the eager ache of this pressing trek,
slithering pools of blankets of rain,
the wealth of the sky gripped every spread
of grass and drip of the fallen twig
so alive with pale greens and softness of the
wavering bark covered wooden limbs.

By this incision of the dark of night,
I fall upon the proud oak tree and sleep into the
posture of purring breath of the falling
Sky.

King of the Mustard Seed

In this warmth of the wooden bedroom, I
look upon her and place my lips
upon the beads of streaming sweat which
trembles across the soft cheeks
of her, silently alive.

Within the curve of her, I became king of
the mustard seed and a perfect
loose grip which scatters quiet life upon the earth,
waiting for the touch of the cleanest raindrops.

Radiant, the plum trees tossed shadows masked by the hues of purple;
I stood silently thinking of her as the juice
trickled down my chin and lips.

By nightfall, many moons past, I recall the
groaning lungs of her as the sweats
of the evening grass bit the sole of these boots.

With the slant of the Summer rain, I could smell the wooden planks
as they tossed dust which filled these old struggling lungs.

Cove

Into the passions of the foamed edges of this heavy cove,
now purified in all my nakedness, I wade into the coolest water
as the skies breeze and sweet laughter tangles upon us.

I spoke to her in the carving press of the ivory flesh which glazed.

In From the Falling Rain

On towns edge, the chapel sang in crackling chants of the bells
which smashed at the hour of noon and all surrounding warmth
paused upon the film of this sweat and green grass fertility.

With slander, I shout to the opening, dark, gray marble sky;
this ivory white cotton shirt, pastes upon my skin,
I open to the slapping canvas which draws in perfect water
born of the hot, seething brand of the sun.

The earth surrenders in sloping dances of the slithering mud.
upon reaching the dwelling of vapors and
mist, I rest on the wooden pew;
with a slashing fever, steam flickers from my scalp and tender flesh.

I return to the fields, meadows and slight glance of the forest,
the burning of the incense of the sweet
flavors, the chapel trims the wind
in an eager push.

White Petal

Roaming among the delicate fragrance of
the grotto of the cherry blossoms,
soft blending winds stroke upon the white petals as I sweetly observe
the rising dust from the hardness of the early Spring fabric of the earth.

On the fracture of the skies fabric of morning,
I witness the resurrection of once fallen clouds which rise as fog.

I claim passage to the winding pass and visit the hyacinth which
grows upon the peak of the Blue Mountain.

Upon the stance on the top of the eastern stroke
of morning blood seething the flank
where endless hues glaze before me, I find a white petal on the edge
of my shoulder and I toss it upon the scar of the earth.

Receding to the Soils of Night

Gentle pearls of trembling clarity soothe
upon the tip of my quivering tongue.

After I hear the speech of the gems of the
shattered glazes of the evening sky,
upon finding me beneath the spread of the tallest red maple,
pouches of the suspension of every leaf holds and covets the pearl.

From the quickness of the falling rain,
blankets of heaviness slope into black flavors of the sweeping sky.

There stood cleverness and charm in the threshing dance of the wind.

In the depths of the hollow night, I resolve
each within the soft soils of the earth.

Migration

Earth rose upon itself as the softest wash of sweet rain
tugged the leaves which fell as a fleece of the
perspiration of the Autumn touch.

From the soothing glazes of the flavors and taste of the rosebush,
I felt hot blood course and travel through the pump of my veins.

After hearing the smack of a distant rain which
travels a heavy course from the endless
curve of the earth, I swim in perfect sight as morning blends
to the disguise of the evening flood.

When Winter slithers it's icy tongue,
I travel south into the furthest reaches of the warmth and heat,
blossoming upon the finest buds and flocks
where the woods coddle chirp and caw.

Goblets and Creek

The pouches of her breasts held as a fine goblet of pale white;
I reached upon the silks of her hair as the
sweet scents wildly dashed upon me.

I walked her into the deep of the down bed
and opened this cove which flooded
the persuasion and timed perfection upon
the rise of the ocean foams.

Beyond the lilies and the slight brown dirt
fleece which hugged beneath you,
I watched you fumble in shaking hands as
the pond giggled in deception.

These bending Summer night notes and I wander
to the motions of the gripping wind,
with a gush of the smacking forest breath, I became
coated with the petals of the woodland trees.

Upon kissing her on the slender neck, I
softly knelt to the pouring creek.

Days in the Park

On the threaded wood of the park bench,
I watched the breath of the grass and the grass
roots waver fog and thin slithering air
crawl to the dampness of the Summer draft.

With solidarity, the thin sleeve of the maple fell in a sweep
and clung, cleft upon the buried bones of my edged shoulder.

By the middle of the bashful decline of the sinking
sun, tremored in a pause and glance,
I slept through the dancing rain which shed like blankets and quilts.

Into the depth of the rise of the moonlit flickering leaves,
the drip of the maple and these quivering dewdrops,
I breathed the milks of Summer air and all humble fragrance.

Dash of the Gazelles

With thick leather, these boots caress the
joust of the tender, moist meadow.

The lilac and the sweet mumbling moans of the quivering roses,
toss and endless fragrance upon the swift and tender wind.

I reach you upon the dense fallen log which pounds against dirt
and humbles upon the dampness of the hollow of the pit.

We sit and watch the gazelles dash through the
clays and crust of the surrendering earth.

I place my hand upon the surrendering winds
as the dust returns to the shedding valley from which it came.

Into the Bog

I weave through the softest press of the deepest part
of the forest ground, the deepest cover and moss.
Holding close as the vines slung with saunter
across the dark edges of the woods.
Gently, I breathed the quiver and trembling
sauces of the forest grooves of the floor.

Through the smallest specks of the canopy of the treetops, I
burrowed through the deep range of the
quivering ferns, alive in heavy greens.

Speaking leaves twirled and tossed through the
quivering moisture which threaded within
the coves and tug of the depths of my soft lungs.

I lean upon the oldest stance of the hickory tree
and smell, feel the shave of the crumbling
bark which spread upon the softness this cotton shirt.

You passed by with the evening fade of the toss
where the sun groomed and swallowed by the sulking
of the rising moon and the moonlit trees.

She glanced by the posture of the wealth of jousting trees;
with the powdered glaze of her pale white skin,
I walked into the deep reach and angles
where the moisture of the clovers softened
me and softened my shaking feet.

Charms and Flocks

Threading through the slick, sweet moisture of the thin air, I
watched, witnessed a full charm dart through the trees.

Wiping the sweat from each edge of brow, chest and shoulders
upon the faint fleck of birds dashing across the sky, I held the stain
of the raindrops as they soothed upon my
shirt and the silks of my hair.

In the melt of dawn with this race through the Alpine breath, air, I
witness the blackbirds gather and hold their
posture in the mud filled grass and fields.

I hear the hollow chirp of these blackbirds which tug as pepper
slouched upon the sky, meeting each meld of meadow and field.

Into the dampness which thickens beneath
the waist and trembles my knees,
gently I watch charms and flocks of the blackbird
scream upon the ridge of South Mountain.

By the Lake

She fell, clouds slithering upon a calm silent lake.
On shoreside, I stood motionless and teased
by the swab of the mist covered press.

With a slow step upon the grass edges and rock laden jousts,
I listened to the snapping crunch of the wild
blade, stalk and scream of the onion sprout.

I turn with a final look and the stream rose
upon her body and heavy flesh.

Into the sweet fragrance of the pine forest which thickened
with sap and the nectar of the sloping,
cascading aromas, the trebling breeze.

Molding needles curled, coved with the
dampness of my burrowing feet;
with a dashing moment, I look to the sky
and see her in a swollen shape
of the breasts and slipping curve,
alive upon the waist and soon I read the
wheats of her tender fields.

Apple Grove

I slipped into the cotton weave which held soft the quivering
dance of the pouches of milks and creams.

Looking beyond, I see the flesh and burnt red skin of the apple trees
which moan upon wilt of the downward wind.

I place her in the curve of the downward slope which cradles
her in the fragrance of the soft glaze of the earth.

With the softness of the quilt, fallen gently along the threads
of stem and bush along the fistful of needles
which steam to the rising craft of morning,
I breath the spices of her as the blushing cheeks
of her toil in reds of the apple tree.

In the Chyme of Midnight

I polished the pearl glazed beads from your shoulders,
slithering gleam of your neck and chest.

I fell upon you with perfect posture and
gesture as the moonlit showers danced
along the moisture of the bristled heat
where the glint of the solar system
fondled within the beads and droplets.

Fresh flooding sight looks above and
tenderly I watch the canvas, gray
and thick marble perches sweetly in quiet gestures
and the tap of the scattering leaves
loosen upon the cracks of the clays of the earth.

I duck beneath this canopy of towering branches
and sleep in the gush of the skies river.

Cobalts in the Forest

I hooked my toes upon the soft thickness of the burrow
of this tender, dough of every bread which
grooves beneath on the pads
of the depth of the silent earth.

Ducked beneath the great red maple, I listen
to the fracture of the tender sky.

Cobalts smack every edge and cove of this heavy lanced forest;
having paused, I swim through the
dewdrops and all scents of solitude
as the melt of the cottons and denims glaze
on the drain of this swollen grove
of trees and thickets.

In this phantom of the slashing bolts of night,
the rise of the fallen clouds return to the rhythms
of dampness and pangs of every shiver.

Vapors along the Velvet Carpet

Vapors rose from the curve of her narrow trembling shoulders;
soft words flickered from her tongue as the mist webbed and shook
upon the tender blades of the heaviest shade of grass.

With a knot, I slung my boots across the sliding slope of my neck.

The fields suckled as a velvet carpet which
deepened into the soil of the earth.
Into the wild of night, I lathered and unloosened upon you.

The rain fell like needles as the sting of the
opening sky dashed with a pinch,
the sting of every blood drop of the sky suckled upon my veins.

Looking behind and beyond, vapors clutter in fading clusters.

Hickory Tree

With the deep veins of the deep roots of the towering hickory tree,
I leaned upon the carved maps of the rising eaves
of the fluttering branches and leaves.

Looking to the spread of the dancing eastern sun,
I motioned to the burgundy canvas as the
sky opened and flooded upon me.

I stood, then walked and rose upon the sloping
treasures of this emerald pasture
which burned in the hottest grass and
motioned me to the sacred forest.

This chapel, covered in branches and moss,
near the ferns and fallen acorns and
fall of the chestnuts, lay as a quivering
altar so full with the dampness
which flooded in passages of sage and sandalwood;
I burrow on this thin snap of fumbling air and
the ghost of the fallen seething clouds
softly fell upon me and gnashed sharp teeth with the falling rain.

Crown

The crowned hill with cascading mud
slithered in precision to the groove of the deep of the valley.

From the humid dance of the potions of the surrendering earth,
soothingly gripped the slapping rain.

I fell upon the quivering rising roots and
motioned to the marble sky.

The blush of the evening swept the pearl drops into the grass, spread
and quietly absorbed upon the depths of the wildflower and clover.

Now, nightfall, I wander into the moan of the grappling woods.

Warmth

She opened upon me as a flood which tapered my hands
and loosened the fine buttons which revealed you in the crimp
of my tender lips and gently, I listened to
the thud of her beating heart
deeply cushioned beneath her warm breasts.

I felt the shadow beneath the tender moon, casting
long stretching shadows across her perfection
and slight roaming curve.

The sky breathed posture and shook her as the doughs of the oven,
sweet tense flavors swept upon the dancing
ferns, alive in each fragrance
which slithered upon the edges of my touch and sensations.

She softened the trembling trim of her quilt and nakedness
which flooded every grip and tension.

Lilacs

Into the fullness of her sweet, soft and mild breath,
well lathered, I stand coated into the the thick
pollens which pepper me in yellow seeds.

With divot and wild spreads, I thicken my
leather boots through the charm
of the meadow and stern posture of the jousting corn.

I think of her as I pass through the wild madness
of the willow tree and the bloom
of the dancing cherry blossoms, tossing petals upon the breeze.

Climbing the slope of the soft, quivering hills, I
remove every stitch of cotton and denim as
the depths of her tangled across me.

I slept upon her in lilacs as the sweetest flavors polished upon me;
The sliver of the cave of her womb where
the instance of life bloomed,

I swelled into the flavor of life and pressed firm
upon the moisture of the descension
of the spread where the orchid moans across my fabric and flesh.

Eulogy

The bark wavered as a map, deeply I found the roots and thick soil
which quivered amongst itself and held a perfect posture.

I felt the rain as each drop of pearl and
dew sank from the dancing sky,
quivered as the silks of my black hair rattled
across my scalp and softened the pulse
burrowed beneath my skin.

I look at the clouds smashing to the moist earth;
sweet flavors of the sky meshed along the snapping
grass beneath the wedge of my boots.

Looking through the marble haze, the glaze of
this tempest swabbed the greatest of oaks
during the dripping clouds.

From the deep charity of the earth, I smelled the
oils as each pocket and pouch caressed
me with rituals and songs of the ribs tenderly
holding me in moaning treble and pause.

Fields in the Frost of Morning Dampness

Into the ribbons of the restful setting sun,
I soaked through the blushing winds which caressed me.

Morning, the earth softened and hosted a calm
dampness with a softening bloom;
I relished in the caress of the blanketed quilt of the earth.

Well into the sinking sky, I sank slightly
with a moist depress of the soil.

By the drench of the middle of this midday, a trembling bloom
gripped the pasture of my quivering flesh
and held me in the temptations
of the sloping breast which rose above the
damp meadow, fields and flicker of day.

With the host of the rise of vapors which
slithered across the frosted dew,
I suckled the creams which burrowed from the
drenching threads of a gushing glaze.

Quiver of Night

Threads of Autumn fell, draped from the
trees of the woodlands and softened
upon the quiet beds of the motionless traces of the earth.

Through the mounds and gathering of the
flood and dew, glaze where the dashing
winds tossed every leaf into the breads of the crisp, cool grass.

I quivered along the burgundy and soft tans of the earth;
well upon the rise where I wade through the
temptations of the floods and flicker
of the swimming winds which toss and turn.

By the depth of the wavering of the joust of late afternoon,
I fell to the creek and trembled in bathing
waters and coiled my feet along
the grip of the soothing pebbles and rocks.

Now, I quiver into the deepest fracture of night.

Past the Hickory Tree

With opened arms, I climbed the spread of the hickory tree.

Alive with a gentle quiver, the soft winds loosened me which
broomed in chestnut colored hues of my thin silk hair.

I walked through the sparse scattered woods and
lulled upon the bark and deepened roots;
the air thickened across me with patterns of the flesh of the earth.

Sweet stillness of the posture of the pond and floating leaf,
I look upon the gleam of the sun, dancing across the softest water.

With fullness, I carve through the wooden chips and soft grass
as I swiftly reach for the depth of the chiseled woods.

Branch and Twig

I spoke with the slicing, carving press of the gusting wind;
into the scent of sap and the nectar of the wavering fruit trees,
the lush and gash of deep Spring fell upon me.

In witness and swift response,
I suckled upon the scent of the lavender and glaze of the milkweed.

The weeds and tall sprout of the grass, stiff
and resilient to the passing breeze,
stands proud and humble to the emerald shine.

I shake the fine, thin trembling caress of the
dancing, flickering loft of my hair
as the quivering looseness of the sprouts and clovers fill my breath.

Looking upon the lust of the red maple,
I hear the quivering shout as the leaves climb
into the bud and proud stems,
layered across the branch and twig.

Looking upon You

Looking within you, I weave the threads of
the satchel nesting your burrowing
glazes, soft upon the warmth which lay tender and polished.

I pause by the flickering water of the tender creek.

With the sauces and mumbling pebbles at the channels end,
I look upon the slicing water and see the glint of your perfect face.

Entering the width and depth of the limes and
emeralds of the trembling meadow,
I look upon the sloping hills and eagerly, I see the breast of you.

The dancing wind slithers across the chestnut brown of my hair as I
relish in the cool fingers of her falling skies.

Gazelle

With the lather of the cream which thickened from the aloe plant,
I soften my hands upon the paleness of the
breads of breast and tuck of the abdomen.

I wander upon your field of soft and tender wheat;
as I speak with the echo of the moans, the cavern which flickers
through the bust of me, quivering sauces slither
and perch as the early dewdrops.

You thrust as the dart of the sweet threads of the gazelle;
swift, I look to the fur and flesh across the open meadow.

Pausing at the thin narrow creek,
I fill my mouth with the crisp sting as the water floods upon me.

With perfect recollection, the milks of the
doughs which rise and heave,
I suckle the dancing pull of her lips as
caressing wind blooms across me.

Rain Storm

I withstood the smash of the glazing winds;
silent upon the slight flicker of every spear of grass.

You sank upon me, the sinking marble
grays of the deepening clouds.

Walking forward, I held the sap from the maple as I brushed calmly
and the burning burgundy skin motioned to the breathe and dash
while I sank on the tucked meadow of the earth.

Further yet, I entered this cove of wrapping winds and the scream
of the furious sky wrapped across me and held me to a slanted stop.

Molecules

The green moss, green ferns and dark emeralds of the scattered hostas,
I wade through this bundle and thicket as the sweet rain flutters across
the leaves on the canvas and treetop, hammock to the sun.

Far to the western winds, heavy grays and slicing wind drifts
a pepper of the brooming geese which carve their
path across the endless rows of maize
and the spread of the meadows, alive in dampness while the flowers
groom upon themselves.

Naked, I walk through the grasses waist high.
Branches of the wild hickory tree bend and
waver as the wild winds greet
with appropriation of waltzing mass and silent matter.

By nightfall, I glisten in the molecules of the shaking beads of dew.

Rib

Well discarded, I remove the satin glaze of the
weave and burgundy of her blouse.

With the blaze of the lemon sky caressing each
corner, nook and cove of the wild
sanctuary, tender upon this lavish earth, I breath
the soil and loosening touch of the leaves
which swab across the cool press of my skin, blood and bones.

I feel with trembling absence of the fullness of lungs.
Into the deep, I tremble with the atoms I share and the hurried growth
where the grass slithers to the clever dance of the sun.

As the blade of the Winter sky, silent and
sharp, I share the bones of me
and I quiver with the rib which opened upon
the nakedness of her soft caress
and the slice well fed along this quiet pursuit.

Into the furthest stretch of the gardens of the
quivering sky, alive as the goblet of Spring,
I declare with the lathering press of the warm
rain, I feed the stream and lush growth
of the fields, thick and miles long.

Lost

Lost, I wander eager through the thick
shades of every hue of the madness
in the wardrobe of the suspension of the woods.

Well across the hollow of the sweet grip of
the jousting breeze which quivered
the pine trees and shed layers the softest needless
of the softest bedding and floor.

Lost, I felt the pinecones soothe the arch of my feet.
scent of the sap washed upon me as the crackling pines and branches
shook through the thick breath which dove from the sky and slithered
through the tamp and wash of the trees.

By the end of the last day,
I walked upon the stretching meadows
and softly, I felt the tender earth
suckle my hooked toes and heavy heels.

Gingerly, I felt the sun shake warmth across
the paleness of my coddled skin.

Falling Petals

As I carve my way deeply upon the moonlit
terrace and the dance of the white cherry
blossoms, I sit still and feel the glaze of the soft
wind and leaves which scatter along the earth.

Glossed by the kitchen window and tucked
beneath the wood of her perfect house,
I watched the candle flame shudder upon the pane.

Swiftly, I walked to the door of her home as
I looked upon her and deepened
to the gash of life.

I felt the breasts of her which softened as the
white petal soothed and caressed
upon the silent soil and taken by the silent wind.

Kissing her, I danced along the polished breath
which mulled me in the depressed
of the apples, alive and perched upon her.

Wedding Day

Crossing the grotto of the chapel, I smelled the pangs of lust as every poise of tender perfection crawled across me.

Laying the cheek of my soft, tender face, I rose upon the breads of her quivering breasts.

The metallic clang of the churchbell slung through the tender sky;
I shook beneath the blanket and dove to
the cream of the lather and milk
which slipped on the tip of my tongue.

We lay along the gown and fleece which
covered the soothing, cool soil.

Fall of the Quilt

The clouds shifted and fell;
soft quivering fog trembled across the stones
resting in the well dressed meadow, I
shook the chill of a heavy November
night as the moonlight danced.

Drinking rain which pelted at a slant,
I watched the vapors of latest pinch of the
days as they surrounded me,
air thinned as I swam across the oak tree, deep in
the center and rise of the floundering quilt.

Tender, I walked across the blanche of the clovers
and the edge of the tallest spears of grass.

Into the hour of the wicked and the soft lull of dissipation.

Autumn Vapors

Across the sloping hills, wrapped in the depth of Autumn,
the red maple stood naked and alone as the
tree branches rattled and shook,
leaving a burgundy covering of leaves which sweetly enticed.

Afternoon, the fog flickered and flooded
as the tongue of the fallen clouds
trimmed well across the grass and the moaning
breath, alive in a sauntering gasp.

I walked through the tangled meadow and filled
my mouth and lungs with the fragrance
of the quivering breath of falling October.

The mist needled in a pinch as the raw skin
of every patch of my full body
opened as an orchid, free upon the sweeping wind.

I look upon the peak of the sloping hill and the
death of the once breathing green grass,
I waver as vapors through the perfect element of Autumn.

In a Moment

I smell the bones and marrow which upholds the clays and soil,
the rigid bend of the earth.

Now, at the green film of the pond, I
tickle the bend of my feet across
the water and soothe my heel and toe in the wavering kelp.

Nearby, I lean against the spread of the willow
tree and relish upon the quivering
branches which soften the sweat from forehead, chest and back.

I look to the flat layered spread of clouds
and watch the flock of blackbirds
pepper their way to the northern sky.

Opening Skirt upon the Wild Wind

Upon spreading her skirt to the slicing wind,
I watched, heard the top of the tree branches
smack and toss a courting
spread of leaves, falling upon the open ground.

Her warm pale thighs threw every scent as
the wild aroma of Autumn deceased
with caresses and blooming weave of the threads and curling leaf.

I spoke to her of harvest as the fields whimpered and the wind
groomed across the spread of the softest wheat.

With the press of her lips to her abdomen,
I felt the glancing twitch of her soft abdomen
and heard from a distance
the moaning salts of the earth.

Fertility of the Autumn Woods

Watching as the current swept across her while suggestive winds
pressed and tugged against the cottons
pronouncing the fullness of her breasts,
I spoke to the threshing bound wheats tossed
from her in the heaviest aroma.

Swift, she snapped the flesh of the plum
while sweet juices slipped down the edge of her thin lips
and nectar fell across the edge of her slow motioned jaw.

I turned upon the flakes of the cool soil
and sweep of the harvest leaves;
motions of her at the spine creek,
I watched as she pulled upon the plums and
drank deeply from the fresh, icy water.

Slightly before evening, I slandered upon her
with the distillery of my warm hands.

Walking together into the deep of the blanketed woods,
we lay on the quilts of the Autumn leaves
cling and crimp beneath us.

We fall and grip onto the dusts of the harvest rising
from the blooming dirt and loosened leaves.

By the Cabin

I open to the breath of the brine coated sea.

Looking to the northernmost ridge and
I lust for the mountain peak,
their speaks the 'caw' of the crows, passing
by in the swing of the murder,

hiking with the gnarled trail and gentle pause,
I smile upon the cabin of the deepest wood.

With the toss of my vision, I look back and
across the sea threaded with foams.

By nightfall, I walk passed the woven cabin
and rest near the coddling stream.

I hear the ocean waters weave as the soft abdomen
of her, caressing the mountain cliff.

About the Author

Under and within the landscape of nature, Donny Barilla coats the palate of his metaphoric and imagist reach as he uses the tremble of his pen to wrangle upon the fever of his surroundings which flood and weave each page. Donny motions primarily as a poet and uses techniques such as he writes books of short stories and novellas and searches his creativity in multiple arenas fastened through thought provoking paints which slip from word to page to book. Keeping late hours which sometimes bleeds into the rising patterns of the sun, he works in his study keeping an espresso machine close at hand. Here, he allows the softened press of his discipline, awake and aware at each moment. Having placed ninety-four poems in journals and magazines, he also donated twenty three books to libraries, academic and public. Donny took first place in the Adelaide Literary Award for Poetry and has placed on two other occasions. After building a construct of vowels and consonants, the words blend upon the page as he pays due respect to the motions of the English language and passions of poetic touch.